there an english menu? *Sumimasen.* Excuse me. *Omizu onegaishimasu.* A glass of water please.

shimasu. Please bring me this. *Omakase shimasu.* Please bring me the chef's choice.

icious. *Okanjō onegaishimasu.* Please bring the bill. *Kādo de ii desu ka?* May I pay with a credit card?

As always to my husband Frank,
my Mother who taught me to appreciate good food
and to our friends in Japan
with whom we have shared many wonderful meals.

Squeamish about Sushi

Published by Tuttle Publishing,
an imprint of Periplus Editions (HK) Ltd.,
with editorial offices at
2-13-10 Shimo-Meguro, Meguro-ku
Tokyo 153 0064, Japan

Library of Congress Cataloging-in-Publication Data

Reynolds, Betty
Squeamish about sushi and other food adventures in Japan / Betty Reynolds.
p. cm
ISBN 0-8048-3301-X
1. Cookery, Japanese. 2. Japan-Social life and customs. 1. Title

TX724.5.J3 R48 2000
394.1'0952--dc21

00-029907
First Edition 2000

Distributors

Japan
Tuttle Publishing
RK Building 2nd Floor
2-13-10 Shimo-Meguro,
Meguro-ku
Tokyo 153 0064, Japan
Tel: (81-3) 5437-0171
Fax: (81-3) 5437-0755

North America, Latin America
and Europe
Tuttle Publishing
Distribution Center
Airport Industrial Park
364 Innovation Drive
North Clarendon, VT 05759-9436
Tel: (800) 526-2778
Fax: (800) 329-8885

Asia Pacific
Berkeley Books Pte. Ltd.
5 Little Road #08-01
Singapore 536983
Tel: (65) 280-1330
Fax: (65) 280-6290

Printed in Singapore

Squeamish about sushi

and other food adventures in Japan by Betty Reynolds

TUTTLE PUBLISHING
BOSTON · RUTLAND, VERMONT · TOKYO

にほん の たべもの
Nihon no tabemono
Japanese food

Eating in Japan is an absolute delight and one of the great pleasures of living here. But to the non-Japanese eating out can be a confusing experience.

At least it was for me when my husband and I moved to Tokyo in 1994. After living and traveling in Southeast Asia for many years we were used to eating chili peppers with every meal. When we first arrived I considered Japanese food healthy but a little bland, and probably at the bottom of my food chain.

Six years later, as we are poised to return to our native country of America I'm surprised to see that Japanese cuisine has become my favorite food.

7:30 pm

7:45

8:00

Remember- you may not be as limber as your Japanese hosts. Stretch your legs eve

At first we were inhibited by the language barrier, indecipherable restaurant menus and our general lack of knowledge of Japanese food. But soon we realized that our forays out were always an adventure. We received some food we didn't know we ordered and ate some things we never thought we would eat - but usually even the consequences of our mistakes were delicious.

In time as we made Japanese friends, we were treated to unique experiences and incredibly delicious food. This sketchbook is a reflection of those many meals shared. I hope it will help people to better appreciate Japanese food, whether they are dining in Tokyo's Ginza or a local Japanese restaurant anywhere in the world.

Goran Kudasai! Please take a look...

8:15

8:30

8:45

fifteen minutes and don't be surprised if you have to be pried up off the floor!

ポワソン POISSON

そば

しゃぶしゃぶ

天丼

おでん

寿司

ふぐ **Fugu**
this hanging fish means poisonous pufferfish are served inside

The noren advertises the restaurant's name or type of cuisine

のれん **Noren:** A curtain hanging outsi...

Signs
of importance

Choosing a restaurant when you can't read kanji, hiragana and katakana can be a bit tricky. Here are some clues to help you find your way.

Beware of shops with dusty plastic food !

サンプル
Sanpuru
plastic food samples outside represent the cuisine inside. This is extremely helpful for beginners.

ぷら means the restaurant is open for business

あかちょうちん
Aka chōchin
hanging lanterns mean inexpensive eating and drinking places

おでん

いらっしゃいませ
Irasshaimase!
"Welcome!"

If people hoot and holler when you enter it means they are glad to see you.

If however, they cross their arms they mean go away = please return another time.

じゅんびちゅう
junbi chū
(preparation time) please come back later

Close

準備中

メニュー
menyŭ
menus with colored photos are a godsend. You can thank your lucky stars when you receive one ↓

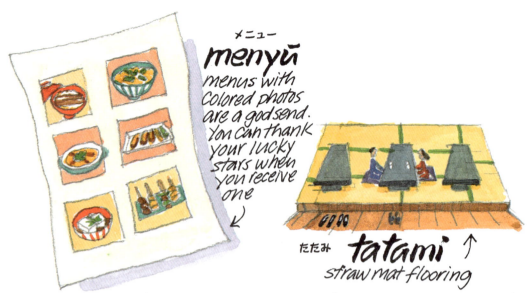

たたみ
tatami ↑
straw mat flooring

おかんじょう
okanjō
Those little pieces of paper (that you can't read) are bills.

Normally you pay on your way out.

Many restaurants have an inner floor called tatami. The Japanese are fastidious about their inner space. It is important to step out of your shoes and onto the tatami without dirtying your socks.

Some restaurants require you to remove your shoes, and change into slippers in the entry way. Remove your slippers at the entrance of the tatami.

くつ
kutsu
shoes
Always take off your shoes or slippers before stepping on tatami. Place them neatly please. Tuck in your shoelaces.

スリッパ
surippa
slippers
step into slippers provided for trips to the toilet.

トイレのスリッパ
toire-no surippa
toilet slippers

Once inside the toilet step into the plastic toilet slippers. Don't forget to remove them when you leave.

"Disorganized shoes are a sign of disorderly thinking" old Buddhist proverb.

Help me please! Where oh where is the toilet?

男 men's toilet

女 women's toilet

おてあらい は どこですか

otearai wa doko desu ka

The only problem with asking this question in Japanese is that the answer will be returned in Japanese.

おてあらい
Otearai
the toilet: another basic necessity

Japanese western style toilets are as talented as they are tricky. Please don't use the control panel unless you are firmly planted on the seat!

At the risk of being too familiar I'd like to explain how to use the Asian toilet. Face inward, straddle the toilet and squat as low as you can. Go slowly to avoid splashing shoes.

Fold in the edges of the toilet paper to show respect for the next person

Some toilets are shared by both sexes

eeek

nozzle on/off

bidet

posterior rinse

nozzle extend

water pressure / high

Dryer temperature

stop!

dryer

nozzle retract

low

お手洗い

ムーブ 入/切

止

おしり洗浄

ビデ

乾燥

前

ノズル調節

後

強

水勢調節

弱

高

乾燥温度

低

温水便座消臭

You can always point to another diner's meal when you can't read the menu

Yes

← the correct way to hold ohashi

Required
Finger skills

Most Japanese meals are eaten with wooden sticks called ohashi. They require a little skill and patience. **gambatte!** (Do your best)

おしぼり
Oshibori
A moist hand towel will be brought to your table

If all else fails— bring your own equipment.

Hey! Where is my soup spoon?

Lift your bowl to your chest. Use the ohashi to eat the morsels, then sip the broth directly from the bowl.

おはし
Ohashi chopsticks

NO!
It is considered impolite to spear your food

Is that person playing a harmonica?

You should never, ever blow your nose at the table but you may clean your teeth with a toothpick.

Just hide the action behind your other hand.

In Japan you always fill your companion's sake cup or beer glass. Never your own.

Hold your cup in both hands to receive.

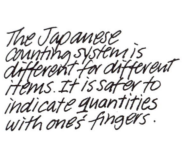

The Japanese counting system is different for different items. It is safer to indicate quantities with one's fingers.

Don't fret if you only receive one big stick— pry them apart at the narrow end.

Waribashi
Half-split chopsticks

You mustn't dig into a central serving dish with your used chopsticks. If there are no serving chopsticks—turn your own and use the thicker ends. (which should be unsoiled if you were paying attention.)

Hold your cup in both hands. The left hand should support the cup

Use your chopsticks to transport the rice to your mouth.

Hold your rice bowl at a comfortable level

When drinking soup hold the bowl to your mouth using both hands. (Don't stick your arms out like propellers)

Don't worry about making a mistake. We foreigners are forgiven almost anything. Just enjoy!

いただきます
"Itadakimasu!"
"I receive/accept this with thanks"

In Japan, even the most humble meal begins with a slight bow and the expression "Itadakimasu". To help us remember this phrase when we were newcomers and unversed in the Japanese language, we were taught the English mnemonic: "Eat a duck I must."

おしぼり
Oshibori
Neatly re-fold after using with the soiled bits facing inward

ちゃわん
Chawan
rice bowl
Soy sauce and food should not be placed on rice

やきものざら
Yakimono
dish for grilled fish

ゆのみぢゃわん
yunomi-jawan
cup for green tea

しるわん
Shiru-wan
soup bowl
Squeeze here to break the seal if the lid is stuck

place lid to the right with inside facing up

Sometimes there is a beautiful design inside.

← My friends make a origami chopstick rest out of the paper case

おはし
← **Ohashi** chopsticks should always point to the left

Sashimi

さしみ

literally
means "fresh slice" — but a more
common definition is raw seafood

おつくり

Otsukuri
creative presentation
of a course of
sashimi

しょうゆ

shoyu
soy sauce

What is considered bait in one country is a gourmet
meal in another. Surrounded by ocean, Japanese
people will put absolutely anything from the sea
into their mouths.
And if fresh is good, then alive is even better!

Sushi すし

vinegared rice

すしおけ
Sushi oke
Container
for serving
Sushi

Sushi or nigirizushi, as it is known here in Tokyo, is an oblong of vinegared rice with a smear of wasabi and is covered with a topping of raw or cooked seafood or some other ingredient. For the novice, sushi is a safer order since it never arrives gasping at the table.

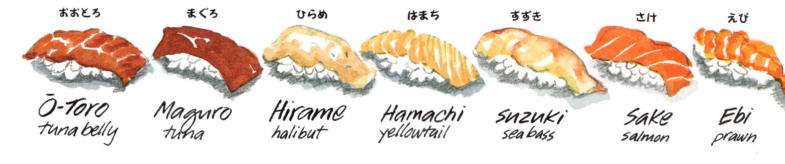

おおとろ
Ō-Toro
tuna belly

まぐろ
Maguro
tuna

ひらめ
Hirame
halibut

はまち
Hamachi
yellowtail

すずき
Suzuki
sea bass

さけ
Sake
salmon

えび
Ebi
prawn

にぎりずし

Nigirizushi
Tokyo Sushi

Sushi can be ordered as a fixed-price set but it is much more fun to sit at the counter and order directly from the chef.

Devotees usually start with an order of sashimi. With sushi they begin with the more subtle flavors of lighter, white fish, moving onto the fattier, stronger tastes. The meal often ends with tamago-yaki (sweet omelette.)

いたまえさん
Itamae san
chef

げた
geta
some sushi chefs wear high platform shoes to keep their feet dry

かずのこ
Kazunoko
herring roe

かつお
Katsuo
bonito

たい
Tai
sea bream

あまえび
na-ebi
eet prawn

しめさば
Shime saba
mackerel

たこ
Tako
octopus

いか
Ika
squid

いくら
Ikura
salmon roe

とびこ
Tobiko
flying fish roe

うに
Uni
sea urchin roe

がり
Gari
pickled ginger

ほたてがい
Hotategai
scallop

とりがい
Torigai
cockle

あじ
Aji
horse mackerel

Agari
あがり
green
Tea

うなぎ
Unagi
eshwater eel

あなご
Anago
sea eel

みるがい
Mirugai
horse clam

あかがい
Akagai
ark shell

あわび
Awabi
abalone

こはだ
Kohada
gizzard shad

たまごやき
Tamago-yaki
omelette

しょうゆ

shōyu
soy sauce

Please use sparingly.
It is considered wasteful
to fill your bowl
too full.

It could also be considered dangerous when you are not skillful with
chopsticks. You could end up with stains on your and your neighbor's clothing.

Sushi tips
I've learned the hard way

It is perfectly acceptable —
and maybe even advisable
to use your fingers.

Dip the
topping
into the
soy sauce

Or end up
with rice
everywhere.

わさび
Wasabi
Spicy Japanese horseradish

あぶない
abunai!
danger!
A little bit goes a long, long way

There are stories circulating about unsuspecting Westerners who have popped the whole wad of wasabi into their mouths and then imploded.

Don't be dainty and try to bite the sushi in half.

ひねしょうが
hine-shōga
grated ginger

がり
gari
Vinegared ginger is eaten between bites to cleanse the palette

べにたで
benitade
flowers of the shiso plant

ほしそ
hoshiso
scrape off downwards and add to soy sauce

eat

だいこん
daikon
radish aids the digestion

きく
kiku
chrysanthemum

しそ
shiso
leaf of the beefsteak plant

don't eat

さいくざさ
saikuzasa
bamboo grass — used for decoration only!

Haven't I seen you someplace before?

Sometimes a piece of sushi has been around the block a couple of times. Check to see if the rice is still moist.

Sit near a sushi chef so that you can choose his freshly-made pieces. If you don't see what you want—ask for it.

You won't receive a bill. Simply wind your way to the cash register (usually near the front door.) You will be charged by the number of your discarded plates.

Plates are color-coded according to the price of the sushi

Help yourself to hot water and teabags

かいてんずし

What goes around — comes around

Kaiten-zushi

Conveyor belt sushi

A fun and less expensive way to eat sushi is to sit at a counter and make your selections from a revolving conveyor belt.

うめしそまき
ume-shiso maki
pickled plum and shiso leaf

なっとうまき
natto-maki
fermented soybean

ねぎとろまき
negi-toro-maki
long onion and raw tuna

サーモンスキンロール
sāmon-sukin-rōru
salmon skin roll

A temaki is rolled by hand

てまきずし
Temaki-zushi
cone shaped makizushi

いなりずし
Inari-zushi
sushi rice in deep-fried tofu pouches

ふとまき
Futo-maki
Large rolls stuffed with pickled ginger, spinach, gour...

Sushi rice rolled in a sheet of nori (dried seaweed) and stuffed with veggies or raw fish with a dab of wasabi

まきずし

Makizushi

makizushi is rolled in a bamboo mat called a makisu

ちらしずし

Chirashizushi

and cucumber.

Sashimi, vegetables, prawns, sweet omelette, fish eggs and other ingredients scattered on top of sushi rice.

たぬき

Tanuki
noodles in hot broth with fried tempura batter

きつね

Kitsuné
noodles and broth with fried tofu and spring onion

つきみ

Tsukimi
noodles and broth with a raw egg

かもなんばん

Kamo-namban
noodles and broth with pieces of duck

Slurp! Slurp! Slurp!

You're supposed to slurp to cool down the hot soup.

Forget everything
Your Mother ever taught you about eating soup! The Japanese way is much more fun.

← You can pick up the bowl and drain the soup.

← You're allowed to stand up and eat at the table.

why isn't anyone waiting on me?

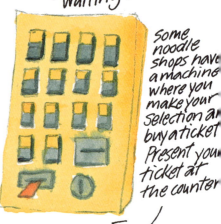

Some noodle shops have a machine where you make your selection and buy a ticket. Present your ticket at the counter.

なべやきうどん

Nabe yaki-udon

Udon noodles and other ingredients cooked in an earthenware pot.

そば と うどん

Soba & Udon
noodle dishes

Most Soba-ya serve soba and udon noodles. Specify your choice.

そば
Soba buckwheat & flour noodles

ちゃそば
Cha-soba buckwheat, flour & tea noodles

Udon wheat flour noodles
うどん

てんぷらそば
Tempura soba noodles in hot broth with prawns fried in Tempura batter

← Often the tables & stools are so tiny that westerners have trouble sitting side by side

やくみ
Yakumi condiments used to enhance the taste

わさび
Wasabi

negi ねぎ

しちみ
shichimi seven tastes spice

Cold noodles are very popular in summer.

ざるそば
Zaru-soba
Cold soba topped with dried seaweed called nori

とっくり
tokkuri
container for sauce

たれ
taré
soy-based dipping sauce

ちょこ
choko
dipping cup

そうめん
Sōmen
Chilled wheat-based noodles are served on ice

ゆとう
yutō
square lacquered container

そばゆ
soba yu
pour the hot broth the noodles were cooked in into your left-over taré and drink like a soup.

ちゃそば
cha-soba
flavored with green tea

もりそば
mori-soba
cold soba served on a bamboo rack in a lacquer box

みそラーメン
miso-rāmen
pork and
vegetables in
a miso-flavored
broth

れいめん
rei-men
cold noodles
with corn,
cucumber,
tomato,
chicken
and
jellyfish

とんこつラーメン
tonkotsu-rāmen
pork and vegetables
in pork and salt-
flavored broth

ねぎラーメン
negi-rāmen
minced meat and
long onion in a spicy broth

ラーメン　らーめん
Rāmen
chinese noodles

カレーラーメン
karē-rāmen
curry-flavored
broth

チャーシューメン

chāshū-men
grilled pork, bamboo
shoots, spring onions
and nori or spinach in
a soy-flavored broth

At last!
A soup spoon

ギョーザ
gyoza
fried
dumplings

シューマイ
shūmai
steamed
dumplings

Hot and delicious, rāmen is taken very seriously here. Everyone has their
favorite soup and is willing to stand in line for it. Rāmen noodles are made
of wheat flour, egg and salt. The noodles are boiled and served in a pork
or chicken-based stock.

てんぷらていしょく

tempura teishoku
A set meal consisting of assorted pieces of tempura, rice, pickles and miso soup

てんどん

どんぶり
domburi
a porcelain bowl for rice dishes

ten-don
tempura and rice with a soy based sauce

An embarassing true story - when I first arrived in Tokyo I confused the dipping sauce for miso soup and promptly drained it. I certainly gave the staff a good giggle.

てんつゆ
tentsuyu

みそしる
miso shiru

いか
ika

きす
kisu

えび
ebi

なす
nasu

れんこん
renkon

dipping sauce

miso soup usually has a lid

squid

white flesh fish

prawn

eggplant

lotus root

てんぷら
Tempura
seafood and vegetables, coated in a light batter and deep-fried until crisp

We filled up on tempura in those early days, since that was something we recognized and could pronounce.

In time we were taken to restaurants where we learned the joy of sitting at a counter, and having hot, crispy morsels delivered piece by delicious piece.

Add the daikon (grated radish) to the dipping sauce or lightly dip the tempura in salt.

さつまいも	しいたけ	かぼちゃ	たまねぎ	かきあげ	ししとう	しそ	アスパラガス
atsuma-imo	shiitake	Kabocha	tamanegi	Kakiage	shishitō	shiso	asuparagasu

| sweet potato | mushroom | pumpkin | onion | lacy pancake | small sweet pepper | beefsteak plant | asparagus |

Food on sticks

Yakitori
やきとり

oroshi おろし
grated daikon with quail egg

しちみ
shichimi
seven-taste spice

Yakitori consists of 4 or 5 pieces of meat, skewered on a bamboo stick, dipped in sauce and grilled over a charcoal fire. Almost every part of the chicken is used in a set course - so if you're not fond of innards it is better to order a la carte.

やきとり
Yakitori chicken thigh

つくね
tsukuné minced chicken

きも
kimo liver

とりかわ
tori-kawa chicken skin

かっぱなんこつ
kappa nan kotsu cartilage

すなぎも
sunagimo giblets

ぎんなん
ginnan gingko nut

ししとう
shishito green, sweet (not hot) peppers

shiitake mushroom
しいたけ

すだち ←sudachi lime

When you order o-makase kōsu (chefs'selection) the food keeps coming until you say "please stoppu!"

しそまき
shiso maki
chicken in shiso leaf →

さけ
sake
salmon

いか
ika
squid

れんこん
renkon
lotus root

アスパラ
ベーコンまき
asupara beikon maki
asparagus rolled in bacon ↑

tako
octopus
たこ

uzura no tamago
quail egg
うずらのたまご

チーズ
chizu
cheese balls

gyū tan
beef tongue
ぎゅうタン

ほたて
hotate
scallop

オクラ
okura
okra

アスパラ
asupara
asparagus

えび
ebi
prawn

Place your discarded sticks in the cup ↓

Kushi-age
くしあげ

Breaded and deep-fried nuggets of seafood, meat and vegetables served with a rich dipping sauce.

Oh no! Do I have to cook that myself?
Being handed a plate of unfamiliar raw ingredients can be intimidating but the staff will be infinitely kind. Act clueless and they will cook it for you.

すきやき
SUKiYaKi

First, melt the suet and grease the pot.

Saute the meat slightly.

Add the stock.

Add the other ingredients a few at a time. Simmer until cooked.

Dip each ingredient into the beaten raw egg.

Raw egg is said to enhance the flavor of sukiyaki.

(Egg shells are free of disease here in Japan)

Do I really have to eat a raw egg?

ほりごたつ
horigotatsu (foot well)

You will probably sit Japanese-style at a low table. Some tables have a hidden well when you can place your legs.

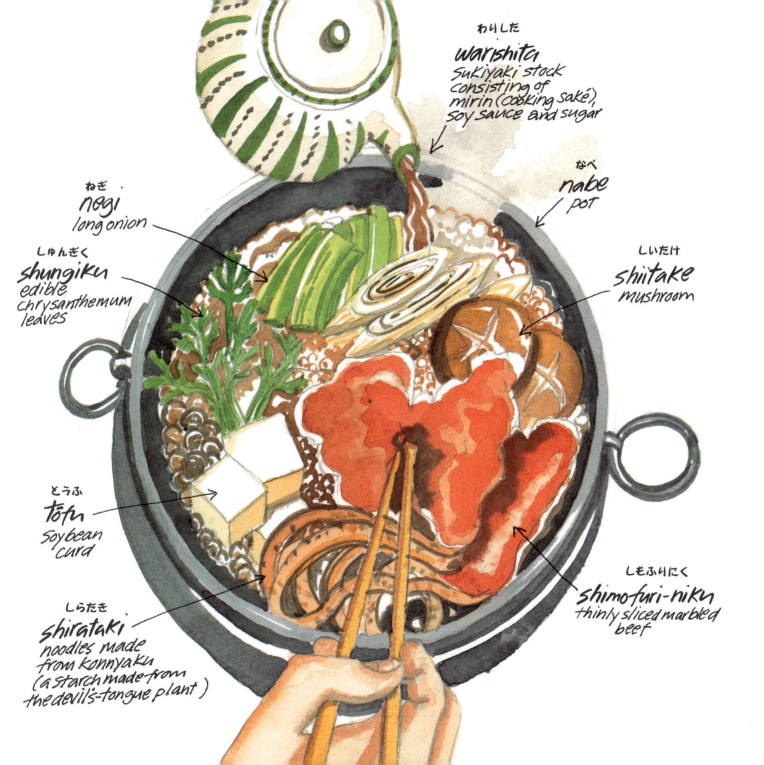

わりした
warishita
Sukiyaki stock
consisting of
mirin (cooking saké),
soy sauce and sugar

なべ
nabe
POT

しいたけ
shiitake
mushroom

ねぎ
negi
long onion

しゅんぎく
shungiku
edible
chrysanthemum
leaves

とうふ
tōfu
Soybean
curd

しもふりにく
shimofuri-niku
thinly sliced marbled
beef

しらたき
shirataki
noodles made
from konnyaku
(a starch made from
the devil's-tongue plant)

ごまだれ
gomadaré
sauce made from sesame seeds, miso paste and soy sauce

ぽんず
ponzu
vinegary sauce made from soy sauce and lemon

うすぎりにく
usugiri niku
thinly sliced beef or pork

しいたけ
shiitake mushroom

やきどうふ
yakidōfu grilled tofu

はくさい
hakusai chinese cabbage

shiratak konnyak noodles
しらたき

ねぎ
negi long onion

えのき
enoki mushroom

shimeji mushroom
しめじ

Periodically skim off the foam with the slotted spoon

だし
dashi
stock made from bonito flakes and kelp

しゃぶしゃぶ
Shabu-shabu

Shabu-shabu is another popular (but expensive) meat dish. Swish the beef into the boiling broth and "Shabu-Shabu". The meat is ready to eat. Dip into one of the sauces. Slowly a the other ingredients, saving the noodles for last.

"No-pan shabu-shabu (no panties) publicize by the financial scanda of 1998 is much more expensive.

These create-your-own pancakes are cooked on a table with a built-in griddle. They are hearty and fun to eat—but don't expect blueberries and buttermilk.

おこのみやき
Okonomiyaki

1. Beat the egg. Combine with flour and water to make the batter.

2. Add your chosen ingredients:

ヤベツ
kyabetsu
shredded cabbage

えび **ebi**
prawn

いか **ika**
squid

ぶた **buta**
pork

agedama あげだま
small chunks of fried tempura batter

3. Pour the mixture on the hotplate. Cook on both sides.

"As-you-like-it" pancake

てっぱん
teppan
hot plate

4. Add the following toppings:

べにしょうが
beni shoga
vinegared ginger

あおのり
aonori
seaweed flakes

かつおぶし **katsuo bushi**
bonito flakes

マヨネーズ **mayonēzu**
mayonnaise

おこのみやきソース
okonomiyaki sōsu
sauce made from ketchup, soy and worcestershire

The choice of Sumō wrestlers
Nabé なべ
Hotpot

Nothing satisfies a big appetite like a big hearty meal. Nabémono is the staple diet of sumōtori. Good for the body—and good for the soul! Especially in winter.

What do Sumo wrestlers eat? Anything they want!

ちゃんこなべ
Chanko-nabé
There are endless varieties of Chanko nabé but the most popular version contains chicken, mushrooms, tofu, potatoes and vegetables simmered in a full-flavored stock.

よせなべ
Yosé-nabé
Contains an assortment of seafood-fish, prawns and clams as well as vegetables.

かきなべ
Kaki-nabé
Fresh oysters and miso paste makes this dish different than the others.

miso

あんこうなべ
Ankō-nabé
Angler fish from the sea are added to the normal ingredients.

なまがき
Nama gaki
raw oysters

やきざかな
Yakizakana
broiled or grilled fish

かいそうサラダ
Kaisou sarada
seaweed salad

てばさき
Tebasaki
grilled chicken wings

でんがく
Dengaku
Konnyaku paste or tofu
broiled with miso

びんビール
bin bīru

なまビール
Nama bīru
draft beer

bottled beer

しろワイン
Shiro wain

あかワイン
Aka wain

チューハイ
chū hai
shōchū and
juice

かんざけ
Kanzaké
warm saké
(rice
wine)

ひやざけ
Hiya zaké
saké
at
room
temper-
ature.

white wine

red wine

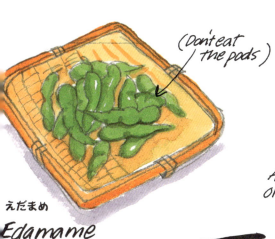

(Don't eat the pods)

えだまめ
Edamame
Boiled beans
in salted pods

おとうし
O-toushi

An appetizer of vegetables
or raw fish will be brought
to your table.

ひややっこ

Hiya-yakko
Chilled tofu

Izakaya いざかや

An Izakaya is a friendly place to eat and drink.
Some are traditional while others are very hip. Sharing
food and swapping stories in an Izakaya is my favorite
way to unwind. After a few beers you are likely to
meet everyone sitting close by.

やきにく

Yaki niku
pork marinated
in soy sauce, ginger,
garlic and sugar

Nasu-no-
dengaku
Eggplant
with miso
sauce

なすのでんがく

The staff will always shout "Welcome" when you enter and "thanks" when you leave. I don't know about
you-but even my Mother doesn't seem this happy to see me!

ばさし

Basashi
raw horsemeat

いか の しおから

IKa-no-Shiokara
spicy, salted squid innards

くじらにく

kujira-niku
some of the whale Killed in the name of research ends up on the menu

ふぐさし

Fugusashi
The toxin from poisonous pufferfish is 275 times deadlier than cyanide.

Enjoy!

すずめ

Suzumé
charcoal-grilled sparrow

さんしょううお

Sanshō-uo
grilled salamander

Please wait until they are very crispy before eating

かぶとに

kabuto-ni
Fish head simmered in soy sauce, ginger, mirin and sugar

the eyes and cheeks are a special delicacy.

Helloooo. Is my dinner still breathing?

Sugata zukuri すがたづくり
Sashimi so fresh it is still moving

Dojō-nabé どじょうなべ
live loach swimming in a pot (until cooked)

いけづくり
Ikezukuri
live seafood and other treats __not__ for the faint-hearted

しらうお の おどりぐい

Shirauo-no-odorigui
tiny live fish swimming in a liquid are meant to be swallowed whole. they quiver the whole way down.

Ebi odori えびおどり
rip the heads off of live prawns and have them dance in your mouth

Iidako いいだこ
Some restaurants specialize in live seafood. Live baby octopus is difficult to keep in your mouth.

めんたいこスパゲッティ

Mentaiko Supagetti
Spaghetti with spicy Cod eggs & seaweed

とんかつ

Tonkatsu
Fried breaded pork cutlet

ミートコロッケ

Mito-Korokke
Minced meat, onion and mashed potato croquette

ボローニャ

Boro-nya
Pizza with onion, hard-boiled egg, corn, minced meat and mozzarella cheese, smothered in ketchup.

つきみバーガー

Tsuki-mi bāgā
Moon-viewing hamburger (A variation on the Egg MacMuffin for the moon-viewing season in September)

Pizza not yet discovered in the Western world.

ビザ

Piza
Pizza

フルーツカクテル

Furūtsu Kakuteru
Pizza with fruit cocktail, cream cheese and cinnamon.

パン

Pan
Bread is always a surprise here when you can't read the labels. I've bitten into breads stuffed with burdock root, salmon eggs, squid ink and fermented beans.

ポテトサラダ
サンドイッチ

Potato-salad sandwich

カレーライス

Karē-raisu
Meat and vegetables cooked in a sweet curry sauce served with rice

オムライス

Omu-raisu
Ketchup-flavored rice pilaf wrapped in an omlette

ハヤシライス

Hayashi-raisu
Japanese beef hash served with rice

When East meets West—

The Japanese will sometimes borrow a dish from another country and then adapt it to make it distinctly their own.
The names of these dishes are written in katakana, the alphabet used for words taken from foreign languages. Pronounce them slowly and you will see the names are familiar to you.

アイスクリーム
Aisu Kurīmu
Ice cream in flavors you'll find only in Japan

Western-size serving

Japanese-size

まっちゃ
Mattcha green tea

くり
Kuri chestnut

さつまいも
Satsuma imo sweet potato

あずき
Azuki sweet red bean

おでん
Oden
and other movable feasts

Delicious food can be found everywhere in Japan.
As a matter of fact - sometimes it finds you.

Oden, much more tasty than it looks, consists of fish-cakes, tofu, radish, eggs and other ingredients cooked slowly in a fish stock. You select your favorite pieces and dip into spicy mustard.

こんにゃく
Konnyaku
devil's-tongue jelly

ちくわ
chikuwa
fish-paste cakes

はんぺん
hampen
fishcake

だいこん
daikon
Japanese radish

たこ
tako
↓ *octopus*

こぶまき
Kobu-maki
kelp roll

たまご
tamago
boiled egg

からし
Karashi
spicy mustard

がんもどき
ganmodoki
fried beancurd

demae
でまえ

Meals on wheels: fresh sushi,
hot noodle soup, pizza and
these food are delivered to
your door. Place the dirty dishes
outside to be picked up the next day.

カラオケビールバス

Karaoke biru basu

Why be bored and frustrated in
Tokyo traffic when you can drink
beer, eat sushi and sing in the
karaoke beer bus?

おでんやたい

oden yatai

Oden stalls open in the evening.
Their light's soft glow looks warm
and inviting.

open ↙ for business

Closed during ↓ the day

いしやきいも

ishi yaki imo
baked sweet potato

The yaki-imo
man sings
to let you
know he is →
around.

だるまべんとう

Daruma bentō
Seasoned meat and vegetables served in a plastic Daruma doll

ぜんこうじべんとう

Zenkōji bentō
Seasonal foods from Nagano

いかめし

Ika·meshi
Simmered squid stuffed with rice.

しゃないはんばいいん

shanai-hambai-in
The employees with food carts usually bow when they exit your train car.

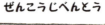

さけ

Sake
rice wine

スナック

Sunakku
snacks of dried squid and octopus

えき

eki
train station

しんかんせん

Shinkansen
Bullet train

うなぎめし

Unagi-meshi
Grilled eel on rice

One of the experiences of traveling in Japan is enjoying the eki-ben (boxed lunch.) Many varieties are sold on the train and in train stations. Wash them down with rice wine, beer or green tea.

えきべん
EKi-ben
Box lunches and other train treats

ミックスサンドイッチ

Mikkusu-sando itchi
An assortment of sandwiches- usually tuna, egg-salad and ham and cheese.

♪ye-sue-koo-reem-moo ♪

アイスクリーム
aisu kurimu
Ice cream is sold in tiny containers

とうげのかまめし
Tōge-no-kamameshi
Rice, chicken, mushrooms, burdock root, bamboo shoot, veggies and boiled egg served in an earthenware container.

きっぷ
Kippu

A dott ¥780

Misspelling on a local train ticket in Kyushu

Irori: Some Inns have irori (open hearths) where your fish and meat are grilled.

しゅんのたべもの

Shun-no-tabemono
Food that evokes the feeling of the season.

Dining and staying over in a traditional Japanese Inn is one of the great pleasures in life but for the non-Japanese it can be a cultural minefield. Just knowing what to do with your footwear requires an education.

Ryokan Ryòri

Japanese Inn Cuisine

にほんちゃ
Nihon-cha
Japanese tea

おしぼり
oshibori
Moist hand towel

おかし
okashi
Japanese sweet

なかいさん
Nakai-san
Your gracious hostess and server will welcome you into your room with tea and a sweet.

Check-in time 3:00 pm

Check-out time 11:00am

Leave your shoes in the entrance way and slip into the slippers provided without dirtying your socks. Leave your shoes below the step.

Your incredibly tiny hostess will insist on carrying your bags to your room.

Leave your slippers in the entry of your room facing outwards.

We westerners tend to hop precariously on one foot-trying to untie our shoes while Japanese slip out of ther shoes gracefully and step up backwards onto the step and into the slippers in one smooth motion.

トイレのスリッパ
toire-no-surippa toilet slippers

ゆかた

はおり
Haori short jacket

surippa slippers
スリッパ

Don't be concerned that your room has no bed. (It will appear later.) Return the bow of your hostess.

Your hostess will serve you Japanese tea and explain the specifics of the inn - in Japanese of course.

When using the toilet-step into the toilet slippers. Please remove them on your way out.

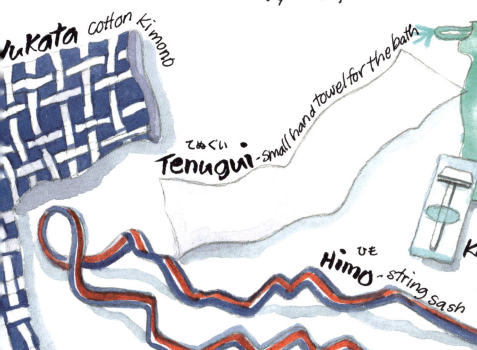

Yukata cotton kimono

Tenugui てぬぐい - small hand towel for the bath

Himo ひも - string sash

Kamisori razor かみそり

Kushi くし comb

ha-burashi ハブラシ tooth brush

Taoru タオル towel

Ha-migaki はみがき tooth polish - actual size

TOiLet PAPER

A change of underwear and socks are the only things you need to pack - everything else is provided.

sometimes the only english words in the whole inn are the only english words you don't need.

Take your yukata, haori, towel and amenity kit with you to the ofuro (bath.) Once again, leave your slippers in the entry.

Place all of your belongings in a basket. Attempt to cover your privates with the tenugui.

Soap yourself up and hose yourself down before entering the bath. Enter slowly! The water is amazingly hot.

ゆ おんな

おんな Onna
woman

ゆ おとこ

おとこ Otoko
man

Caution: make sure you choose the right bath. Women's curtain is usually pink or red. Men's curtain is blue.

f there is a rotemburo (outside
ath) take another long soak
d admire the view.

Dry yourself off back in the
changing room.

Return to your room in your
yukata and haori. Now you
are dressed for dinner.

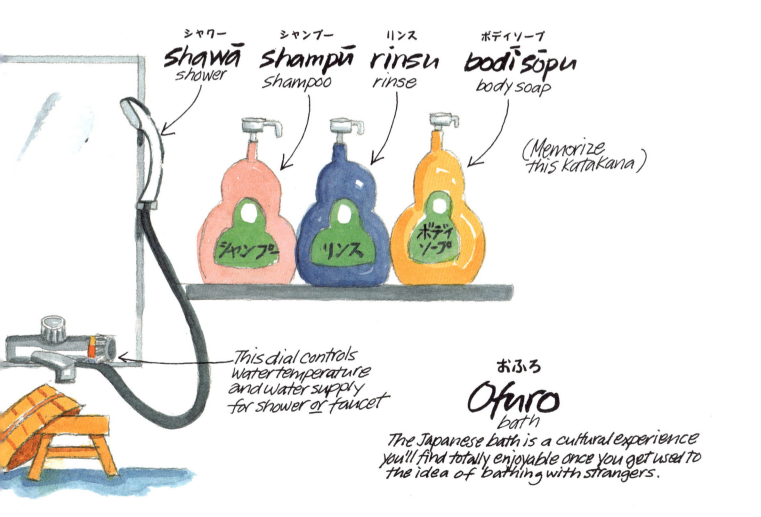

シャワー
shawā
shower

シャンプー
shampū
shampoo

リンス
rinsu
rinse

ボディソープ
bodi sōpu
body soap

(Memorize
this katakana)

シャンプー

リンス

ボディ
ソープ

This dial controls
water temperature
and water supply
for shower or faucet

おふろ
Ofuro
bath

The Japanese bath is a cultural experience
you'll find totally enjoyable once you get used to
the idea of bathing with strangers.

かいせきりょうり
Kaiseki-ryōri
consists of several courses of artistically arranged, delicious seasonal foods but...

(Some of it may be unrecognizable to you.) Often your meals are served in your room.

てんぷら
tempura
deep-fried battered prawns and veggies

てんつゆ
tentsuyu
tempura dipping sauce

さしみ
Sashimi
raw fish and prawn

ごまどうふ
goma dōfu
sesame tofu

にもの
nimono
boiled vegetables and meat

すいもの
suimono
clear soup

うめしゅ
umeshu
plum wine

vegetable hors d'oeuvres
zensai
ぜんさい

ばんごはん
Ban gohan
dinner
(All this food is a serving for one person)

After dinner drag your overly full self to the Karaoke bar to entertain the other guests.

さけ
saké'
rice wine and other forms of alcohol cost extra

メロン
meron
melon

さかなのてりやき
sakana-no-teriyaki
fish broiled with soy sauce, saké, mirin and sugar

なべもの
nabemono
meat, fish and vegetables cooked at the table

みそしる
miso shiru
miso soup

ちゃわんむし
chawan mushi
custard made from eggs and fish broth with delicious things inside.

つけもの
tsukemono
pickled veggies

にほんちゃ
nihon-cha
Japanese tea

ごはん
gohan
cooked rice

The Grand Finale - rice, miso soup, tea and pickles

futon ふとん
Japanese bedding will be waiting for you when you return.

Have a good night's sleep and wake up hungry for a hearty breakfast.

ume boshi うめぼし
pickled plum

gohan ごはん
cooked rice

Ocha おちゃ
green tea

nabe なべ
hot pot with meat and vegetables

sarada サラダ
salad

natto なっとう
sticky fermented soybeans

nama tamago なまたまご
raw egg

nori のり
dried seaweed

himono ひもの dried fish

kamaboko かまぼこ
fish paste

tsukemono つけもの
pickled veggies

あさごはん
Asa gohan
breakfast

miso shiru みそしる
miso soup

いか
ika
squid, squid, squid and more squid. stuffed, fresh, dried and every other form imaginable

つけもの
Tsukemono
pickled vegetables

おみやげ
Omiyage
souvenirs

サンショウウオ
Sanshō-uo

A six-pack of freeze-dried salamander

からし めんたいこ
Karashi-mentaiko
spicy cod roe

わさびのおかし
Wasabi no okashi
cakes & chocolates with pieces of spicy horseradish

...one in Japan would dream of returning home from a vacation or a business trip without ...ying a souvenir of food to show the folks back home what they missed. Coming from a ...ture where a typical gift would be a box of fudge or salt-water taffy - Japanese take-home ...ok some getting used to. After sampling many - I must admit they are tasty.

Mind you don't get run over by one of the many conveyances

Breakfast at Tsukiji

If you are a foodie Tsukiji fish market is not to be missed. My advice is to skip the 5:00 a.m. tuna auction where you'll only be in everyone's way. Wait until 8:30 or 9:00 am when market workers are more relaxed and friendly to casual browsers.

Get absolutely squished against a tiny counter for the most delicious, freshest sushi around.

Or try one of the many food stalls selling hot soup and other dishes. Make your decision quickly or you are likely to be dismissed by the staff!

ひもの
Himono driedfish

かに
kani crab

Katsuo-bushi
bonito flakes
かつおぶし

こんぶ
Kombu dried kelp

たこ
Tako octopus

ひれ
Hire toasted fins from the poisonous pufferfish

せいろう
Seirou steamer

さしみぼうちょう
Sashimi bōchō sashimi knife

おわん
Owan bowls

さんま
Sanma pacific saury

ou can spend hours shopping in the many stalls and shops in the surrounding area

Whole lot of eating going on!

Sumo Supper

Going to the sumo arena is a thrilling cultural experience - not only because of the sport. It is one big picnic for most of the spectators.

かいせきべんとう
Kaiseki bentō
An assortment of cooked and raw treats

パーティーセット
Pāti setto
An assortment of party foods

What's the big party? Why wasn't I invited?

7:00am
Someone from the office is sent to stake out the picnic spot.

10:00am
Mothers and children take their places.

11:00am
Office workers beg

おにぎり

Onigiri
rice balls
wrapped
in
nori

うなじゅうべんとう

**Unajū
bentō**
grilled
eel on
rice

やきにく

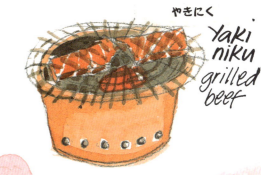

**Yaki
niku**
grilled
beef

はなみ

Hana mi
Cherry blossom-viewing party

The beautiful cherry blossom season in early April is a magical time.
In Tokyo it becomes one big, week-long excuse to party. Eating
portable foods and drinking saké while viewing the blossoms has
been a tradition since ancient times.
   Look longingly at a party in progress and you'll probably
be invited to join in. If not—you can always start your own.

Kampai!
Cheers!
カンパイ！

arrive.

7:00 pm
Serious partying begins

10:00pm
Many parties are at a feverish pitch.

やきそば　たこやき　とうもろこし　お好み焼

あゆ
Ayu
grilled
Japanese
river trout

まつり
Matsuri
Festival

やたい
← **Yatai**
street stalls

Traditional festivals called Matsuri are connected to the agricultural calendar. No festival would be complete without the sights and smells of the many colorful food stalls lining the streets.

Yatai snacks are eaten while standing on the pavement—one of the few times it is acceptable to do so in Japan.

はちまき
← **Hachimaki**
head wrap

はんてん
Hanten →
short
coat

じかたび
**Jika
tabi**
split toed shoe
socks →

やきそば
Yaki soba
chinese noodles with vegetables and meat

たこやき
Tako yaki
pieces of octopus cooked in flour and egg

おこのみやき
Okonomiyaki
Japanese pancake with vegetables, meat or seafood

かきごおり
Kakigōri
shaved ice with fruit-flavored syrup

みこし
Mikoshi
A portable shinto shrine paraded through the streets during festivals

チョコバナナ
choko-banana
chocolate-covered banana

みたらしだんご
Mitarashi dango
rice flour balls coated with sweet soy sauce

みずあめ
Mizu ame
sugar coated pickled plum

やきいか
Yaki ika
grilled squid

とうもろこし
Tomorokoshi
grilled corn dipped in soy sauce

はつもうで

Hatsumōde
The first visit to a temple or shrine is a time to pray for prosperity in the coming year.

しめなわ

Shimenawa
Sacred ropes of rice-straw are hung at Shinto shrines to separate the pure world from the impure.

おしょうがつ

Oshōgatsu
Japanese   New Year

The first three days of January have the invigorating feeling of festival. Many businesses, restaurants, food stores and museums are closed so it is a great time to people-watch at Buddhist temples and Shinto shrines.

もちつき

Mochi-tsuki

You will see people pounding rice to make mochi.

はまや

Hamaya
Demon-quelling arrows

あまざけ

Amazaké
sweet sake is sold at yatai

Jūbako
じゅうばこ

Osechi-ryōri is served in a tiered lacquer box called a jūbako

Otoso
おとそ

Sake, with seven special herbs is served to every member of the household.

Osechi-ryōri
おせちりょうり

Beautifully-prepared, home cooked food is eaten on the first three days of the New Year. The ingredients represent harvests from the fields, the sea and the mountains.

Nishimé にしめ
creatively-carved boiled vegetables

Kamaboko かまぼこ
Boiled fish-paste cakes

Kazunoko かずのこ
Herring roe is a symbol of procreativity

Tazukuri たづくり
small fish symbolize a good harvest

Ebi
えび
prawns symbolize long life.

Kuromamé
くろまめ
Black beans represent good health

Toshikoshi soba
としこしそば

symbolizing long life is enjoyed by families on New Year's Eve before they set out to visit a temple or shrine.

Ozōni
おぞうに

A special soup containing mochi is eaten on New Year's Day

Chew the mochi carefully - so that you don't choke,

and end up as a New Year fatality.

はる
Haru
Spring

なつ
Natsu
Summer

あき
Aki
Fall

ふゆ
Fuyu
Winter

わがし
Wagashi
Japanese Cakes

みずようかん
Mizu-yōkan, a type of jelly eaten chilled in summer ↓

Kuri くり
chestnut

むしようかん
Mushi-yōkan is a mixture of An and wheat flour which is steamed in a mold.

とびん
Dobin
earthen teapot

Traditional Japanese cakes are very different from Western ones. Namagashi (uncooked cakes) are made from wheat flour, rice and a paste of sugar and beans, sweet potatoes, or chestnuts called An.

Namagashi are beautifully designed to match the seasons of the year. They must be eaten soon after purchasing.

Wagashi can be bought in department stores and speciality stores called Wagashi ya.

さくらもち
Sakura-mochi

Rice dumplings wrapped in cherry blossom leaves are eaten on Doll's Festival Day (Hina Matsuri) March 3rd

かしわもち
Kashiwa-mochi

Rice dumplings and sweet beans wrapped in oak leaves

Both are eaten on Children's Day (Kodomo no hi) May 5th

ちまき
Chimaki
Rice dumplings wrapped in bamboo leaves.

おはぎ
Ohagi
Mochi wrapped in sweet bean paste is served during Spring and Fall Equinox

だいふく
Daifuku
A thin layer of mochi is wrapped around sweet bean paste

Monaka
もなか
A double wafer filled with sweet bean paste

くしだんご
Kushi dango

Rice balls on bamboo sticks either coated with An or soy sauce.

たいやき
Tai-yaki
pancakes filled with An and baked in molds

Imagawa-yaki
いまがわやき

ていしゅ
Teishu
Tea Master

まっちゃ
Matcha
powdered green tea served during the tea ceremony

ひがし
Higashi - Dry sweets eaten before drinking matcha

てやきせんべいや

Teyaki sembei ya   *Rice cracker shop*

ビール
Biru
Beer

← My favorite food group

かきピー
Kaki-pi
crescent-shaped rice crackers with peanuts

おせんべい
The noisy snack

Osembei
Japanese rice crackers

Try one piping hot and freshly dipped in soy in Asakusa or Kamakura.

Teyaki
sembei
てやきせんべい

ざらめせんべい
Zarame sembei
sweet rice crackers also have a slightly salty taste

えびづくし
Ebi Zukushi
prawn cracker

There are basically two types of Japanese rice crackers— savory and sweet. Savory sembei are made by steaming rice flour. Then they are baked and brushed with soy sauce. Sweet sembei are made from wheat flour, sugar and glucose.

Sembei come in all sizes and shapes and can fill a whole aisle in a supermarket. They are delicious with green tea or cold beer.

Note: sembei can have a distinctive odor you may find unpleasant when you are not the one eating them.

What is that weird smell?

Kyūsu are difficult to use if you are left-handed

とうがらしせんべい
Tōgarashi sembei

Flavored with hot pepper— very spicy!

きゅうす
Kyūsu
Small teapot

しながわまき
Shinagawa-maki
Roll-shaped rice crackers wrapped in seaweed

あげせんべい **Age sembei**
Fried rice crackers

あられ **Arare**
small rice crackers

ごませんべい
Goma sembei
have a sesame taste

ごちそうさまでした
"Go chisō sama deshita"
"Thank you very much for the delicious food / drink"

After a meal it is polite to bow and say "go chisō sama deshita" to your host or chef.

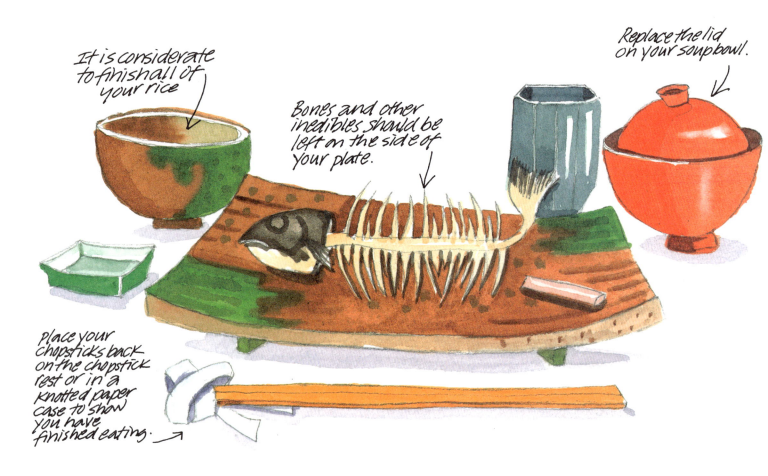

It is considerate to finish all of your rice

Bones and other inedibles should be left on the side of your plate.

Replace the lid on your soup bowl.

Place your chopsticks back on the chopstick rest or in a knotted paper case to show you have finished eating.